MUMMIES

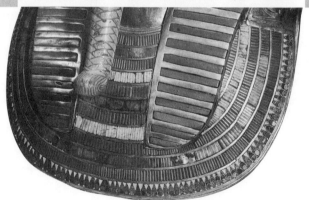

DANA WHITE

GREAT SOURCE
EDUCATION GROUP
A Division of Houghton Mifflin Company

S0-CWS-494

Reading Advantage Authors
Laura Robb
James F. Baumann
Carol J. Fuhler
Joan Kindig

Project Manager
Ellen Sternhell

Editor
Jeri Cipriano

Design and Production
Anthology

Photography and Illustration
Front cover, p. 7 © Thomas Hartwell/Corbis; pp. 1, 53 © Mike Lawn/Fox Photos/Getty Images; p. 6 © Charles & Josette Lenars/Corbis; pp. 11, 18, 32, 47, 55, 59 map art by Sue Carlson; p. 12 Courtesy of Nevada State Museum; p. 15 © Sharon Long, as the artist of facial reconstruction, and Chip Clark as photographer/Smithsonian; p. 18 © Three Lions/Getty Images; p. 20 © AP Photo/Martin Mejia; p. 25 © AP Photo; p. 29 © Mike Lawn/Evening Standard/Getty Images; p. 31 © Bettmann/Corbis; p. 33 © Eurelios/Phototake; p. 35 © Corbis SYGMA; pp. 37, 40, 43 © Giansanti Gianni/Corbis SYGMA; p. 47 © Historical Picture Archive/Corbis; p. 49 © Stapleton Collection/Corbis; p. 51 © A. R. Coster/Topical Press Agency/ Getty Images; p. 52 © Mansell/Time Life Pictures/Getty Images; p. 55 © AP Photo/University of Pennsylvania Museum of Art and Archaeology; p. 56 © Keren Su/Corbis; p. 58 © AP Photo/Dolkun Kamberi, University of Pennsylvania Museum of Archaeology and Anthropology

Printed in the United States of America

International Standard Book Number-13: 978-0-669-51417-9

International Standard Book Number-10: 0-669-51417-9

4 5 6 7 8 9 10 – RRDC – 10 09 08 07 06

CONTENTS

Chapter 1 What Is a Mummy? 5

Chapter 2 Spirit Cave Man
(North America—Nevada) 10

Chapter 3 Juanita, the Ice Maiden
(South America—Peru) 17

Chapter 4 Lindow Man, Yde Girl
(Europe—England, Holland) 27

Chapter 5 The Ice Man
(Europe—Italy) 34

Chapter 6 King Tut
(Africa—Egypt) 46

Chapter 7 Taklamakan Mummies
(Asia—China) 54

CHAPTER 1

What Is a Mummy?

Suppose you were asked, "What is a mummy?" You might give an answer similar to the following:

"Mummies are dead people wrapped in bandages. They rise from their graves and walk around. They scare the living daylights out of people. Some mummies put an evil curse on anyone who crosses their path."

Well, that's partly right. That is what some *movie* mummies do. But there is one thing movie mummies and real mummies have in common. Mummies are dead people whose bodies have been *preserved,* or saved. Some bodies were treated and preserved on purpose by humans. Other bodies were preserved by nature, whether by accident or because humans used nature to preserve bodies.

The bodies are not just skeletons. They still have their skin. Sometimes they still have their organs inside and muscles, too. In fact, some real mummies almost look alive.

This is a mummy of an Inca child. He looks as if he might wake up at any moment. But he is dead, frozen in time.

Despite the fact that some real mummies look alive, they won't rise from the grave unless someone lifts them out. Real mummies don't walk around. If they scare people, they don't mean to. If people fall down dead after seeing a mummy, those people probably had something wrong with them to begin with.

The Making of a Mummy

The way a real mummy looks depends on how it was preserved. The ancient Egyptians were masters of mummy-making. They *embalmed,* or treated a body so that no bacteria or fungi could grow on it and destroy it. (Bacteria or fungi normally break down the tissue around the bones of a dead body.)

Embalming was done to preserve the bodies of the great pharaohs for the afterlife. The Egyptians had learned to remove the organs and dry a body with a kind of salt. There were several more steps taken to preserve the body with oils and other things, and then it was wrapped in linen. The mummy was buried in a coffin, which was sometimes placed inside another coffin. Then it was placed in a tomb with the pharaoh's possessions.

The Egyptians mastered the process of preserving bodies.

Another ancient people, the Incas of Peru, also mummified their rulers. The rulers were wrapped and placed in royal tombs along with food, cloth, and weapons. People and animals were also sacrificed and placed in the tombs.

The Egyptians, Incas, and other early peoples preserved some of their common people, too. But the common people did not get royal tombs. The people were simply buried in places where bacteria and fungi could not grow, or they were buried in soil full of chemicals that killed bacteria and fungi. Some bodies were buried in snow and ice on high mountains. Other bodies were buried in peat bogs—wet, spongy, swampy areas—where there is very cold water and little oxygen. (Bacteria and fungi cannot grow without oxygen.) Still other bodies were dried by fire or simply buried in the hot, dry sands of a desert.

So now you know a little about mummies that were made on purpose. But some bodies also became mummies by accident. Whether the people died accidentally or were murdered, nature took care of their bodies over time. Icy mountaintops, for example, are natural freezers!

Stories to Tell

Mummies have been found all over the world. We know why these dead bodies survived for thousands of years. We also know a little about the times in which many of the mummified people lived. But we don't have the answers to all the mysteries about them.

Come step into the world of some famous mummies. Maybe one day you will help solve one of the mysteries about them.

2

Spirit Cave Man
(North America—Nevada)

About 10,630 years ago, a man died. He may have died of a fractured skull. Badly infected teeth may also have led to his death. He was about forty-five years old and stood five feet two inches tall. He had black hair.

When he was buried in a dry cave near Fallon, Nevada, a prehistoric lake nearby was just starting to dry up. Knowing that explains part of his funeral clothes. He was wrapped in mats woven of bulrushes. (These are tall, grass-like plants that grow in wet ground along a shore or in shallow water.) He also had a robe of rabbit fur and well-made moccasins. His grave was shallow—only two feet deep. His body mummified naturally in the small, dry cave.

Discovery in 1940

Archaeologists Sydney and Georgia Wheeler had been hired by the state of Nevada to explore and excavate the cave that the state called "Spirit Cave." The couple discovered the mummy in Spirit Cave in 1940. He became known as Spirit Cave Man.

Near the mummy were found woven bags and everyday artifacts (tools and other things he had used). A couple of bags held the ashes and bone fragments of two other people. They had been cremated, or burned.

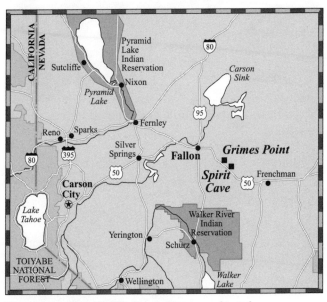

The area where Spirit Cave Man was found

The Spirit Cave Man's burial spot helped to mummify his body.

Experts thought the mummy was two thousand years old. That would fit with the diamond-shaped pattern in his bulrush mats. That pattern was thought to have been developed by people living about two thousand years ago. The mummy was brought to the Nevada State Museum. He was put into a closed wooden box for over fifty years.

Fast Forward to the 1990s

The Spirit Cave Man find was published in a report by the Nevada State Museum in 1969. However, the next dealings with the mummy didn't happen until 1990. That's when a federal law, NAGPRA (Native American Graves Protection Repatriation Act), was passed. It aimed to stop the removal of Native American bones and artifacts. The Paiute-Shoshone (PIE yoot-shaw SHAW nee) tribe claimed Spirit Cave Man as a relative because he was found on land where their ancestors had lived.

The 1990 law required federal agencies to look at museum collections of human remains. If the remains were tied to modern Native American tribes who claimed them, then those remains must be returned for reburial. Nothing else was done at this point, however.

In 1994, new technology allowed for a carbon dating of Spirit Cave Man. This showed that he was about 10,630 years old. Researchers at the Nevada State Museum consider him to be the oldest mummy found in North America and one of the oldest in the world. His skull is not like those of modern Indians. The closest matches are the Ainu, the original people of Japan and other parts of Asia.

Over the next several years, a number of things happened with Spirit Cave Man. University and museum archaeologists asked permission to do tests on human remains at the Nevada State Museum. Spirit Cave Man was included. Indian leaders refused. They said the tests would invade a living body. They believed the spirit stays with the remains and that disturbing the remains also disturbs the souls of the dead.

In 1998, a forensic, or scientific, artist made some head models of Spirit Cave Man and another mummy. But state officials said that the heads couldn't be displayed. State officials had to wait for a decision of who owned the remains. It was finally recognized that the Bureau of Land Management—the BLM—had the final decision-making power. In 1999, the BLM told Indian leaders that Spirit Cave Man was not tied to modern Nevada tribes.

In August of 2000, the BLM decided that Spirit Cave Man was not Indian and that the U.S. government owned him. However, no further testing was permitted.

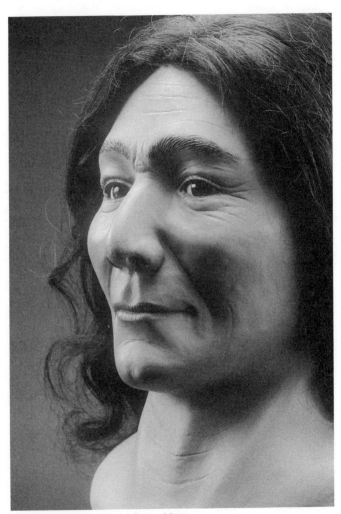

A clay bust of Spirit Cave Man

Who Owns a Mummy?

The question of who is the rightful owner of a mummy is sometimes very tricky. Countries all over the world have had to deal with this situation. Is it "finders-keepers?" Does science own the mummies? Do people have the right to claim them as ancestors? Or do mummies deserve the respect and privacy of their graves? Does anyone at all have the right to disturb them?

Even if a decision of ownership of a mummy has been made, studying a mummy can sometimes destroy it. Some famous ice mummies, for example, started to melt and decay as soon as they were uncovered.

As you probably realize, people will continue to deal with questions of ownership and respect concerning mummies. And people will continue to find them and study them. After all, mummies are a key to unlocking our past.

CHAPTER

3

Juanita, the Ice Maiden (South America—Peru)

In September 1995, two climbers on Mount Ampato faced a life-or-death situation. They were on the highest peak in a section of Peru's Andes Mountains. The descent to their camp was treacherous, and they had little more than an hour of daylight left. They were worn out, and one of them, Dr. Johan Reinhard, an archaeologist, was sick. Earlier, he had melted some ice and drunk it, and it had made him ill.

Earlier in the day, Reinhard and his companion, Miguel Zarata, had found an ancient Inca ceremonial site near the summit, or top, of the mountain. The Inca once ruled most of the western length of South America. The ceremonial site was where the Inca offered human sacrifices to their gods. (The Spanish arrived in 1532 to conquer and destroy much of that culture, but Inca Indians still live in the Andes.)

Machu Picchu

At the ceremonial site, the men had found a small Inca building. The building was a tomb that contained a mummy wrapped in a bundle of cloth and some statues made of gold and silver.

Everything was covered in ice. But the men knew that the bundle was a mummy from the way it had been wrapped. Other mummies wrapped like it had been found in that area before.

A Priceless Mummy

The men were more than twenty thousand feet high, and they were lightheaded because of the lack of oxygen. To make matters worse, the air was full of choking ash blowing up from an active volcano below.

Reinhard knew that even if the mummy was partly thawed, it was priceless. Only three frozen South American mummies had ever been found. The mummy in this bundle might be the fourth.

The ice around the statues and bundle had melted a little during the day in the sun. As the day ended and the sun was setting, the bundle had frozen tight to the ice beneath. Zarata voted to leave the frozen mummy there and return the next day. Reinhard had not decided himself what to do.

Before the men could decide, something else happened. The stone walls of the small Inca building on the summit shifted. Part of the building slid down into the mountain's volcanic crater. The tomb had slid down into a crater now filled with spears of ice. One spear of ice had halted the mummy's slide, but for how long?

An experienced climber, Reinhard knew that if they left the bundle, it could slide further down and be lost. Or a snowfall could make it impossible to find the mummy again.

Zarata used his ice ax to cut the bundle loose of the ice. He turned the mummy to get a better grip—and both men looked into the face of a young girl! They were stunned.

The mummy was later named Juanita, the Inca Ice Maiden.

The men then faced a big decision. If they left the mummy there, they would need a government permit to come back for it. Getting a permit would take weeks or months.

As day turned to night, it began to snow. Then the volcano below them erupted, so Reinhard made a decision.

Saving the Mummy

Reinhard tucked the statues from the summit into the top pocket of his backpack. He also picked up other artifacts found on the slippery way down to the mummy bundle. Reinhard and Zarata then wrapped the mummy in plastic and attached it to Reinhard's backpack. The backpack was very heavy.

Wearing headlamps, the men traveled a mile to go around the ice before they hooked up with the trail to their camp. Every time Reinhard slipped, he crashed to the frozen ground. In order to get up, he had to prop his ice ax on the ground and lunge to his feet.

Once away from the ice, the path was even more treacherous. Zarata went ahead to chip footholds. Both men could have been swept off the mountain at any moment.

The men then faced another problem. Their headlamps dimmed. Finally, at 19,900 feet, the men carefully hid the mummy behind some ice and inched down the last seven hundred feet to their camp. It took them two hours.

The next day, Reinhard returned to collect the mummy. Zarata took the rest of their equipment to their base camp. He then brought a burro and a driver back to meet up with Reinhard.

The men wrapped the mummy in insulated sleeping pads to keep it from defrosting. The burro driver covered the burro's eyes to keep the animal calm as they went further down the mountain.

When the men arrived at a village, they loaded the mummy into a bus's cool undercarriage. Then they headed for a city university where there was a freezer and other scientific help.

At the university, the mummy was named Juanita. Her parents would never have named her Juanita because it is a Spanish name and the Spanish had not yet arrived when "Juanita" lived. Nevertheless, that was the name scientists gave her.

Juanita's Messages

Juanita had many stories to tell the world. The beautiful Inca burial cloth frozen to her skin contained much information for textile (cloth) scientists.

Another "message" involved DNA that had never been known before. DNA determines what color a person's eyes or skin will be and much more. The DNA variant in the Ice Maiden said it was probably possible to find girls in today's Peru who are related to her!

Ritual Sacrifice

Part of Juanita's story has to do with sacrifice. The Inca thought the mountain gods protected them. They believed that the gods sent rain for the crops and brought order after disasters like earthquakes or an emperor's death.

The perfect, beautiful children sacrificed to these gods brought honor to their families and villages. The children were the best the people had to offer, and the children were willing to die.

A sacrifice was a sacred ceremony that took place on the highest possible place, often above 17,000 feet. The only written accounts of this ritual are from Spanish historians.

First, a child was chosen or offered to the emperor. Priests led a procession from the child's village to the emperor. There were huge ceremonial feasts. Then the priests led a procession to the chosen mountain. Llamas carried supplies like stones, grass, and soil to a base camp. Buildings to shelter the priests and the child were built there.

At the same time, a tomb was built on the summit. Burial artifacts like carvings of llamas, small statues, and ceremonial pots went into the tomb. These would go with the child to the Other World.

Some scientists think this child was struck on the back of the head. Juanita had a skull fracture. So do most of the skulls of other sacrificed children. Johan Reinhard feels this was to help them escape a slow, painful death.

After the child's death, priests returned to the site to make other offerings to the mountain gods and to fill the tomb with dirt.

More Clues to the Inca

Johan Reinhard made another expedition to the Andes the year after Juanita was found. He found several more ice mummies. All were children.

In 1999 and 2000, a whole town of mummies came to light. About 2,200 mummies of all ages and classes were discovered in an Inca burial ground near Lima, the capitol of Peru. These were not ice mummies—Lima is on the dry, sandy coast of the Pacific Ocean. But they lived at about the same time as Juanita.

After scientists finish studying the mummies, the mummies will go to a museum. Perhaps these mummies will explain some of the mysteries that still surround the Inca. One of these is the knotted strings called *khipu* (KEE poo). They may be decoded to tell scientists even more.

Spanish conquerors knew the Inca kept business accounts with khipu. But they were not sure what else the strings recorded. So they destroyed many of them.

A Spanish historian tells of travelers who met an Inca man who tried to hide the khipu he carried. When questioned, the Inca said his khipu was a record of the acts of the conquerors. The Spanish travelers burned the khipu and punished the man.

In 1997, a burial site in northern Peru contained thirty-two intricate khipu. Strands hanging from the horizontal cord had their own strands. Some of these secondary strands had another strand attached.

Some experts today say khipu were just business tools. Others say they were memory aids for a culture that did not have a written language.

But a new theory says the knotted strings *are* a written language! The knots are binary codes like the eight-digit sequences of 1's and 0's used by a computer. Khipu, says this expert, is based on a seven-digit sequence.

Another mystery!

Lindow Man, Yde Girl (Europe—England, Holland)

Andy Mould worked in Lindow Moss, a peat bog (wet, spongy ground) in England. On August 1, 1984, he and another man were cutting peat into blocks to send to a shredding mill. (Peat is used for gardening and for burning as fuel for heat.)

The day was a normal day until Mould saw a chunk of wood in a peat block. He tossed the block to his coworker. The peat fell and crumbled. The piece of wood turned out to be a dark brown human foot! The machine being used to harvest the peat had cut off someone's foot!

Finding a foot could have been a shock. But pieces of people often turn up in peat bogs. In fact, the year before, Mould had found a woman's head.

Mould knew that he had to call the police about this find. This foot could be the foot of a recent murder victim.

Police arrived. Mould and his coworker showed them where they had found the foot. Further searching led to a piece of darkened human skin. Like the foot, the skin had been "tanned" by acids in the bog.

The foot and skin were covered with wet peat, and scientists were called in. Newspaper and TV reporters soon showed up, too. They called the mummy "Pete Marsh" because it had been found in a peat marsh. (It was a bad joke.) Others were more serious. They named the mummy "Lindow Man."

A cutting machine sliced off a slab of peat. The aim was to get the whole body. Unfortunately, someone misjudged where the body was. The machine sliced off the rest of the mummy's legs. The peat holding the rest of the mummy's rubbery body was taken to a hospital for examination.

Examination of Lindow Man

Just looking at the mummy told investigators they had a murder victim. X-rays confirmed it. Lindow Man had been struck twice on the top of the head and once at the base of the skull. The blunt weapon used was probably an ax.

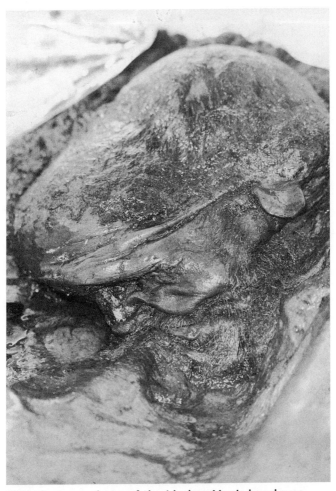

This close-up photo of the Lindow Man's head was taken at the site where he was found.

Lindow Man had also been strangled with a rope. But he had not drowned. His throat had been cut before he went into the bog. Cutting his throat drained his blood.

Investigators wondered if Lindow Man had died in some kind of ritual. When the remains were dated, investigators were more intrigued. This shocking murder was committed two thousand years ago!

Who Was Lindow Man?

Lindow Man was unusual because he had a beard. No other bearded bog man had ever been found. His hair had been trimmed with scissors days before he died. Few people in England had scissors then.

Clothes tell a lot about people. But this mummy was naked. He wore only the rope around his neck and an armband of fox fur. The bog had decayed the rest of his clothes. So Lindow Man could have been rich or poor. His hands were not calloused or scarred, so he had not been a working man or a warrior.

How tall had Lindow Man been? One forensic test uses the length of the leg bones to find a person's height. This test would not work with Lindow Man. His legs were gone. So forensic scientists, people who use science to solve crimes, used another measure—the length of his upper arm bone.

The scientists determined that Lindow Man had been about five feet, seven inches—taller than most men of the time. Examination of his teeth revealed that he was between twenty-five and thirty years old.

Lindow Man's preserved stomach held some grains. He had eaten just before death. Some of the grains were burnt. This led to a theory about his identity.

The theory suggests that he was a priest of the Celts. The Celts were fierce warriors. They also farmed a little. Important men had beards or a moustache.

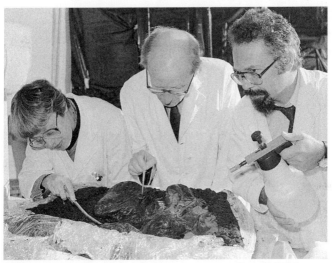

Studying Lindow Man raised many questions about who he was.

The Celts sacrificed people to their gods. They believed this would bring good fortune. In one ritual, victims "chose" themselves by eating a bit of burned bread from a plate.

The Celts believed bogs were powerful links to gods, goddesses, or dead relatives. Celts threw offerings like pots, jewelry, and even whole wagons into the bog. A sacrificed person was a powerful offering.

Most bog bodies come from Northern Europe. Most died violent deaths. That was true of another bog body found in 1897 near the town of Yde in Holland.

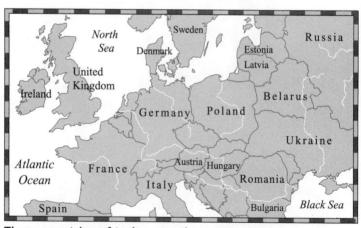

These countries of today are where many bog mummies died centuries ago.

Yde Girl

Her darkened body rose from the bog headfirst. Her hair was red. Workmen thought they had found a demon . . . or that a demon had found them!

Yde Girl was sixteen when she died sometime between 170 B.C. and A.D. 230. She had been strangled and stabbed. Examination showed she had scoliosis. This is a physical condition in which the spine is curved. She may have walked with her right foot twisted slightly inward. But why had she died? Usually, only perfect sacrifices were offered to honor the gods. Her life and death remain a mystery.

Yde Girl, as found and reconstructed

CHAPTER
5

The Ice Man
(Europe—Italy)

On September 19, 1991, Erika and Helmut Simon
were hiking in the Alps—the mountains between
Italy and Austria. The Simons came upon a trench in
the rocks that was filled with glacier ice and melted
water. That was to be expected. The last few
summers had been warm, so the glacier was melting.

That's probably why the Simons found something
they did not expect—a corpse. The corpse's head
and upper body stuck out of the ice. The Simons
thought they had found a hiker who had had a bad
accident. They reported their find to a nearby lodge.

The owner of the lodge thought the body was just
an unlucky hiker, too. Many hikers had had accidents
and fallen into the glacier. Their bodies would then
turn up thirty or so years later. Nevertheless, the
lodge owner notified the authorities.

The discovery of the Ice Man

The next day, an Austrian rescue team arrived by helicopter. They also thought the corpse was just another lost hiker. And they thought their job was simply to free the corpse from the ice. In their rush to get the job done, they made mistakes.

Recovery Attempts

The recovery team tried to pry the body loose with a stick they found. Then the rescuers tried to pull the body free by tugging on its clothes. The clothes shredded. One man used a power chisel on the ice and accidentally drilled a hole into the corpse's hip.

To be fair, the recovery team was forced to work in bad conditions. They stood in icy water. When the weather worsened, the team gave up for the night. They took a handled axe blade from the site to prove the body was over one hundred years old.

The next day, two rock climbers stumbled upon the body. They lifted the head and checked out the clothes. They found other artifacts, but they did not want to destroy evidence.

By now, rumors of the find were flying. Was the body a victim of crime? A few days later, forensic scientists from the University of Innsbruck claimed the body. A complete examination would follow.

By the time the scientists arrived, the cold nighttime temperatures had frozen the body back into the ice, and it was covered with a fresh blanket of snow. It took much effort with ice picks and axes to get the body free. On the ground, the body was forced into a coffin, breaking its left arm.

The mummy became known as the Ice Man, sometimes called Oetzi for the area in which he was found. The Ice Man was helicoptered out in a body bag with all of his belongings. Then the body was brought to Innsbruck, Austria, in a hearse.

At the morgue, photographers and television crews took pictures. The Ice Man began to defrost. A fungus spread across his skin. Quickly, he was put into a freezer.

The Ice Man was thought to be four thousand years old. Later research added on more than a thousand years. The 5,300-year-old Ice Man became a sensation all over the world.

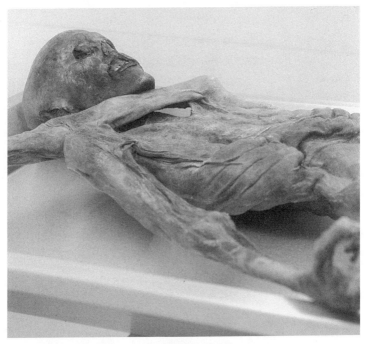

Finding the Ice Man was a landmark discovery.

Who Owns This Mummy?

As mountainside excavations went on, Italy and Austria fought over the Ice Man. The border was officially resurveyed. The survey showed the Ice Man's find spot to be in Italy, but by less than three hundred feet. The Province of South Tyrol in Italy claimed property rights.

Nevertheless, the University of Innsbruck was allowed to study the Ice Man for three years. While the Austrians did that, the Italians built a grand new museum. The Ice Man has been in that museum for years now in a special refrigerated unit.

In early 2003, the Simons filed a lawsuit. They wanted to be named the official discoverers of the Ice Man. On November 3, 2003, the court decided they were.

The Ice Man's Real Value

The 5,300-year-old mummy is one of the most studied mummies in the world. The reason is that he wasn't buried. He died in his everyday clothes with his everyday equipment. This is important.

This evidence is invaluable in understanding the time between the Stone Age and the Neolithic Age.

Many artifacts were found with the Ice Man. These included a bead with rawhide strings and two dried mushrooms on leather straps. Clothes of finely stitched animal skins included a goatskin coat. And part of a boot stuffed with grass for warmth was still attached to one foot.

An excavation of the site in October of 1991 resulted in more artifacts. These included a nearly intact arrow quiver, or case that holds arrows, and the remains of birch bark containers and their contents, which included pieces of fur and leather, bits of a net made of grass rope, and flints.

Other excavations uncovered more leather, grass, and fur. The Ice Man's fur cap was found, along with bits of his skin and muscle tissue. There was also hair and a single fingernail.

Botanists (plant scientists) added their clues. An ancient wheat came from washing the Ice Man's clothes. The wheat had been processed, or threshed. That meant the Ice Man had been in contact with farming people.

This is a reconstruction of how the Ice Man looked.

The Ice Man's Story

What were some things the scientists learned? For one thing, the Ice Man had done a lot of walking. Signs of frostbite and bone wear pointed to an active, outdoor life in the high, cold Alps.

The Ice Man knew how to survive in changing weather and confusing, thick fogs. His grass cape was waterproof. He wore his tools on his belt. He had a lightweight frame backpack. His arrows were hunter's arrows and he carried replacement parts. He could obviously fix things.

But the Ice Man was no superman. Patterns in his recovered fingernail showed that he had been seriously ill sixty, eighty, and one hundred twenty days before he died. His arteries had hardened. (Arteries are part of the body's blood system.)

But there was also evidence that he had tried to take care of himself. He had several cuts in his skin that had been filled with herbs. Then the herbs were burned. Something like charcoal may have been rubbed into the wound. That irritated the skin and left a mark—a tattoo. The tattoos and the Ice Man's other artifacts say astonishing things about medicine more than five thousand years ago!

Ancient Medicine

Were the Ice Man's tattoos some kind of ancient acupuncture chart? Acupuncture is an eastern therapy, a way to heal. Very thin needles are put in key places in a person's skin to adjust energy flow in the body.

The Ice Man's tattoo scars may have been a way to get longer-lasting healing. Or the tattoos may have been meant as a chart to help others know how to relieve his pain.

Further study showed that the tattoos were not placed by guesswork or for decoration. Some ancient healer had tattooed a cross on the Ice Man's left ankle and a "master point" on his back. Pressure applied on these two tattoo spots at the same time are known to ease rheumatism, a painful joint or muscle condition.

There were fifteen groups of tattoos on the Ice Man's back and legs. Eighty percent of the points match the points used in modern acupuncture.

When he died, the Ice Man wasn't feeling well. His stomach hurt and he felt weak. He had whipworms. Remember those dried mushrooms on a leather thong? They turned out to be a kind of fungus containing oils that kill worms. The mushrooms helped the body flush out the worms and their eggs.

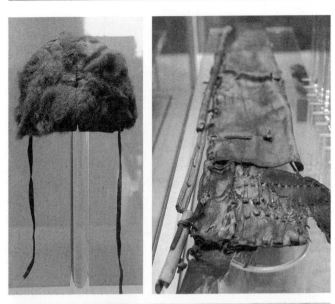

Studying the Ice Man and his possessions has provided many clues about his time.

The Day the Ice Man Died

The latest theory about the Ice Man comes from scientific advances made in 2003. It provides more details about his last day.

The Ice Man was forty-five years old. He had never gone farther than thirty-seven miles from where he was born. His birthplace was an Italian village close to where he was found. But he spent most of his life in a valley farther north.

His last day probably seemed promising to him. He had two meals. One was near a small Alpine village. He drank some water and sniffed in pollens from the aromatic pine forest there. He had some wild goat meat and bread made with wheat and herbs.

The "bread" was more like a tough cracker than bread as we know it today. Tiny bits of charcoal in the bread showed that it had been baked on a hot rock or next to a fire. The Ice Man might have baked it himself, as hunters often do.

More than likely, the Ice Man had one or more companions with whom he climbed the mountain. They would hunt wild goat and antelope. And they'd be hunting in dangerous border territory. They climbed, then stopped for another meal— this time, red deer meat and the same bread.

Hunters from another territory found them. For maybe four days, they fought a deadly fight. The Ice Man took an arrow in the back. He was cut on his hands, wrists, and rib cage. The wound on his hand was savage. The arrow in the back was deadly.

DNA blood tests on the Ice Man's weapons and clothes show that four people besides him fought. Bloodstains on his goatskin coat show that he carried a wounded companion for some distance.

At some point, someone must have pulled the arrow from the Ice Man's back. He could not have done that himself. But that didn't help him.

The blood on the Ice Man's weapons reveals that he shot at least two different people and retrieved the arrow each time. Then he shot again—and the arrow shattered.

Time ran out. The Ice Man stacked his belongings neatly. Was he alone now? Had his companion or companions died? Then he lay down, and the snow came.

The Ice Man probably never knew he would leave such archaeological riches. He probably only wanted to survive. But at the end, he had been hurting and alone when he died. Only future study will show if this theory is correct.

CHAPTER

6

King Tut
(Africa—Egypt)

Howard Carter, an Englishman, had a dream. His
dream began in 1882 when he was eight years old
and saw an exhibit about Egypt. He was hooked!
He decided that he would devote his life to
studying Egypt and mummies.

Carter's Dream Comes True

When Carter was seventeen, he found a way to
make his dream come true. He got a job working
in Egypt as a tracer. A tracer copies tomb paintings
and inscriptions onto paper for others to study.
Carter's father, an artist, had taught him to draw.
That was all the education Carter had. It was
also enough!

The next year, Carter went to work for a
famous archaeologist who trained him professionally.
Carter went on archaeological digs and made
several important finds. He also learned the
Arabic language.

After that, Carter continued to work at digs. All his hard work paid off when he was twenty-five. The Egyptian Antiquities Service asked him to supervise and control archaeological digs in the Nile Valley.

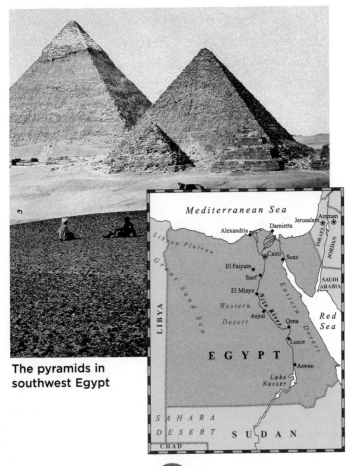

The pyramids in southwest Egypt

All went well until some French tourists attacked Carter's men. The tourists wanted to get into a dig. Carter did not stop his men from fighting back. The tourists complained to powerful friends. Carter's superiors ordered him to apologize, but he wouldn't. As a result, Carter was demoted to an unimportant job. Carter tried to make that work, but he couldn't. So he resigned. For two years, he painted watercolors and guided tourists.

Carter, Lord Carnarvon, and King Tut

In 1908, Carter's luck changed. He met Lord Carnarvon, a wealthy Englishman. The two started working together in the broiling heat of Egypt's Valley of the Kings.

While in the Valley of the Kings, Carter's dream grew bigger. He had seen the name of King Tutankhamen on artifacts. Now Carter was determined to find the king's tomb.

Lord Carnarvon said he would fund Carter's search, and he did. But by June 1922, Lord Carnarvon had spent about two million dollars. Lord Carnarvon funded Carter's search for one more season. After that, Carter paid the workmen himself and went on.

King Tut Found!

All of Carter's work paid off on November 4, 1922. That day, his men were shoveling rubble at the base of the tomb of Pharaoh Rameses VI. They found a step cut into the rock cliff. Carter knew most tombs in the valley had stairways. The men dug further and found more steps. Carter notified Lord Carnarvon, who came as soon as he could.

Lord Carnarvon, Lady Evelyn, and Howard Carter stand at the entrance to the tomb of Tutankhamen.

By November 24, sixteen steps had been dug out. Lord Carnarvon and his wife, Lady Evelyn, had joined Carter. Now, in front of them was a doorway. It was plastered and sealed. Carter knew that it could mean it was the tomb of an important person.

There were signs that part of the door had been opened and reclosed. Carter and Lord Carnarvon figured that ancient tomb robbers had entered the tomb. (Many tombs had been raided in ancient times.) Block by block, the men broke down the stone doorway.

Behind the doorway was a sloping passageway full of more rubble. It took two more days of work to clear the passageway. This tunnel ended at another blocked door. But on this door were the royal seals of Tutankhamen!

Carter noticed that part of this door had also been opened and then closed with a patch of plaster. He chipped away at the covered hole and made a new hole. Lady Evelyn handed Carter a lit candle, and he put it up to the hole. He looked through and saw shapes and shadows and the glint of gold. As his eyes adjusted to the light, he caught sight of statues and wooden animals covered in gold.

At about 4 PM that day, Carter, broke through the final door. He entered a tomb that had been silent and dark for more than three thousand years. Lord Carnarvon and Lady Evelyn followed him.

The treasures that they saw left them speechless at first. And it was not just one room. There were three rooms completely filled with vases, furniture, statues, and more.

These are treasures from the first room. Two life-sized statues are of a king. Their headdresses, skirts, and sandals are made of gold.

When Carter and other members of the excavation team finally got to the room where King Tut was, they were astounded. They opened one coffin after another until they got to the third coffin. This inner coffin was solid gold. It held the mummy of King Tut, perfectly preserved and wearing a jeweled gold mask. The artifacts are now in museums in Cairo and Luxor, Egypt.

Today's scientists are sure that King Tut died at the age of seventeen or eighteen. But they do not know how he died. Some people think he was killed. Others think he may have died from an accident. We may never know for sure.

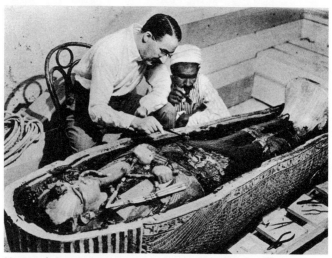

Howard Carter examining the coffin of Tutankhamen

This was Tutankhamen's (King Tut's) death mask. It is made of solid gold.

7

Taklamakan Mummies (Asia—China)

In the late 1980s, people began finding perfectly preserved, three-thousand-year-old mummies in a remote Chinese desert. They had long, brownish-blond hair, European features, and didn't appear to be the ancestors of modern-day Chinese people. Who were they?

For Victor Mair, they were the mummies of people he might meet at a family reunion. Mair, a scholar of Chinese literature, is Caucasian. He was guiding a learning tour in China. He took his group to the Provincial Museum of Urumchi. The museum had a new archaeology exhibit. Mair left his group to take a look. And for the next three hours, he forgot all about his tour group. He just stared at the mummies.

The mummies had been reclaimed from the Taklamakan Desert near the towns of Cherchen and Loulan. These towns are in the Tarim Basin, which is ringed by rugged mountains.

The area where the Taklamakan mummies were found

A body is found in the Gobi Desert, China, which is in the Tarim Basin.

Explorers cross the Taklamakan Desert. Archaeologists now think the mummies may have been the citizens of an ancient civilization that existed at the crossroads between China and Europe. The mummies are called by several names, depending on where they were found and where they are now in museums. The mummies are called Taklamakan mummies, Cherchen mummies, Tarim Basin mummies, and Urumchi mummies, just as an example.

The mummies were far more lifelike than Egyptian mummies. They were so perfect that Mair almost thought they might be a trick, a hoax. Yet he felt a strange sense of kinship with them.

Dry climate and salt deposits in the desert had made these mummies. They had brownish-blond hair. Their coloring plus their deep-set eyes and long limbs indicate that they had a Western European heritage.

Had these people been here forever? Or had they migrated from somewhere? If so, from where? And why? Scientists have different answers to these questions.

Where Did These Mummies Come From?

Clothes often offer clues. But in this case, they pose more questions. The mummies wore wool felt with stamped patterns. Other clothes had been beautifully woven from strands of sheep's wool dyed bright colors. The woven patterns were tartan plaids and twills. Celtic societies like those of the bog bodies had worn similar patterns. Chinese looms at the time were made only for silk.

Had settlers from the west brought wool-weaving looms? Some of the Tarim Basin mummies looked Celtic.

**A well-preserved mummy of a
woman still in all of her clothing**

Some scholars think that the mummy people
migrated through central Eurasia to the Tarim
Basin. But one scientist has a different idea. His
name is Dolkun Kamberi.

Kamberi is an archaeologist. He recovered the
mummies in the exhibit that Mair first saw.
Now Kamberi and Mair are working with other
scientists. They want to save as many Tarim
Basin mummies as possible. And they want to
solve the mysteries of those mummies.

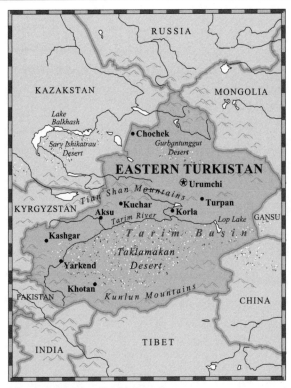

Map of Eastern Turkistan

Kamberi grew up in Eastern Turkistan. He is Uygur ("we-gar"), the native people of the area. As a child, Kamberi heard folk stories about non-Chinese settlers in the area. He also heard stories about foreign archaeologists who came in the 1800s. These scientists found graves, art, and manuscripts of a highly developed culture.

But these facts still do not say who the mummy people were. Kamberi thinks he knows. A native Uyger, he has medium-brown hair. His face is not Asian. He thinks his history is the same as that of the Tarim Basin mummies. He also thinks the Tarim Basin people have been in the region since prehistory. Learning the history of those people will rewrite *world* history, Kamberi says.

Nearly a thousand mummies have been reclaimed from the desert. Some are Chinese-looking Mongoloids. In some graves, Mongoloid and Caucasoid bodies are buried side by side. Other mummies look European.

Clues to the Mummy People

You have read about some of the clothing clues to the origins of the mummies. Here is another. Mair collected three felt caps. One is from a village in southern China. The second is from his grandfather's village in Austria. The third is from the Tarim Basin. *The caps are identical.*

The early Tarim Basin people raised sheep, cattle, and horses. They farmed. They wove cloth. They used wheels. They built round houses. They thatched the roofs with river reeds.

These early people lived in oases along the desert's edges. Farmers still live in these areas of green. These farmers have little contact with the world. Their tools and methods are like the old ones.

Evidence from graves that Mair and his coworkers have been allowed to excavate confirms the farmers' isolation. So do bodies and artifacts found in out-of-the-way museums. In one small museum, Mair found 3,200-year-old *cowrie*— seashells. The sea is thousands of miles away with lots of baking sand in between. These ancient people had to trade over long distances!

Burial Practices

Information about these early Tarim Basin people has been gained from studying the mummies and the clothes and artifacts found with them. The artifacts suggest what their daily lives might have been like.

The artifacts also provide clues to the burial practices of the people. For example, an infant recovered by Kamberi was buried with a leather baby bottle. Was that to give the baby a sense of comfort? Another baby found was buried with blue stones on its eyes. Was that to show how the baby looked when it was alive? There are no clear answers to these questions.

Mummies found in some graves suggest some chilling burial practices as well. Mair and a Chinese official found the mummy of a woman on top of the sand, above a burial tomb. The official said this young woman was sacrificed for the occupant of the tomb. The official said that her eyes were gouged out. Her arms were broken off at the elbow and her legs yanked out at the hip. If this is true, the young woman had a horrible death.

A baby buried in a hole below the woman found on the sand also had a horrible death. The little boy was eight to sixteen months old. He had been held up by the legs and buried alive. Traces of tears are still on his face.

A few other burial practices seem to be connected to religious practices. Symbols found in other graves show the people worshipped the sun, the bull, and the horse. A horse's skull and leg were found in some graves. The ritual meaning of this is not clear.

In another mystery, excavators found a saddle cover and a pair of strange pants in a grave. On one pant leg was a picture of a blue-eyed human. On the other leg was a horse with a human hat. No one knows what these symbols mean.

What Lies Ahead?

Old Chinese books describe tall figures with deep-set blue or green eyes and brownish-blond or blond hair. These bearded "hairy ones" looked like monkeys to the ancient Chinese. Scholars once laughed at the stories. Mair thinks they should be re-examined.

Sand moves over the graves of the mummies. How many mysteries are yet to be discovered? Only time will tell.